Exploring Sectarian Opportunities in the Middle East

A Monograph
by
LTC Bernard K Hill
United States Army

School of Advanced Military Studies
United States Army Command and General Staff College
Fort Leavenworth, Kansas

AY 2011

Abstract

Exploring Sectarian Opportunities in the Middle East by LTC Bernard K. Hill, USA, 40 pages.

Since the death of the Prophet Mohammad sectarian violence has existed in the Middle East. This monograph details the history of the Sunni - Shia split and explains the origins of the violence still present today. This conflict presents opportunities to Western governments and militaries to explore in the operational and strategic realms. Two dissimilar case studies, Yemen and Syria, are used to recommend engagements to exploit these opportunities. Both of these countries have existing or potential sectarian violence and clear tensions between the Sunni - Shia sects.

Yemen has a sectarian insurgency led primarily by members of the Zaydi Tribe who were the former ruling party. The Shia Zaydi feel marginalized and targeted by Sunni extremists and al-Qaeda elements with-in Yemen. Western militaries must use the advisors already engaged in Yemen to convince the GoY to initiate the amnesty, reconciliation, and reintegration process in Yemen. This will undermine al-Qaeda initiatives in Yemen and, hopefully, build a bond between Sunnis and Shias creating a stronger, more stable governance structure.

Syria is governed by a Shia minority. Western governments' isolationist policies toward Syria have pushed the Syrian minority government to become overly reliant on Iran. With the introduction of a new American Ambassador to Syria operational opportunities are present that have not existed in many years. Military to military exchanges, foreign military sales, and theater security cooperation exercises are ways western militaries can begin to exert influence in a country with which the American government and military has had little or no interaction. Leveraging a Sunni majority could help the United States to apply its national power in a positive way to shape the Shia minority government and drive a wedge between Syria and Iran.

Table of Contents

Introduction

On 22 February 2006 in Samarra, Iraq, north of the capitol city of Baghdad, a terrorist attack occurred at the al-Askari Mosque also known as the "Golden Mosque."[1] The al-Askari Mosque is one of the most revered holy sites for Shia Muslims and it serves as a mausoleum to the 10th and 11th Imams, Imam Ali al-Naqi and Imam Hasan al-Askari, respectively.[2] During the attack twin bombs were placed inside the dome, destroying the iconic landmark, however, there were no reported casualties.

The effect of that single act of terror caused the sectarian violence in Iraq to increase so dramatically that, within one year, there were reports of more than 3,000 civilian deaths each month.[3] President George W. Bush stated on 06 March 2007:

> Last February, al Qaeda and other Sunni extremists blew up the Golden Mosque of Samarra. This atrocity was designed to provoke retaliation from the Iraqi Shia - and it succeeded. Radical Shia elements, some of whom receive support from Iran, formed death squads. And the result was a tragic escalation of sectarian rage and reprisal. This changed the nature of the conflict in Iraq. We still faced the threat from al Qaeda, but the sectarian violence was getting out of hand, and threatened to destroy this young democracy before it had a chance to succeed.[4]

This wave of sectarian violence had a profound and gruesome effect on Operation Iraqi Freedom. Coalition Soldiers on patrol in Iraq during the height of the sectarian struggle frequently encountered the handiwork of individuals carrying out reprisal killings. Soldiers often found men with gunshot wounds to the back of their heads and bound with handcuffs or wire.

---

[1] Global Security.org. "Samarra", John Pike, http://www.globalsecurity.org/military/world/iraq/samarra-mosque.htm (accessed November 18, 2010)

[2] Ibid.

[3] Burns, John F., "Efforts to Avert Sectarian Reprisals After Shrine Attack" *New York Times*, http://www.nytimes.com/2007/06/14/world/middleeast/14iraq.html (accessed November 14, 2010)

[4] Bush, George W. "*The War and Caring from American Soldiers: Remarks at the American Legion 47th National Conference*", Presidential Rheroric.com, http://www.presidentialrhetoric.com/speeches/03.06.07 html (accessed November 18, 2010)

For the destruction of an iconic building to trigger such great violence, it was clear that powerful individual motivations were at play. Although sectarian violence in Iraq had slowly been rising before this event, the reason behind the massive spike in violence was unclear. How did the violence get so out of control? With this basic question in mind, this monograph will explore the idea beyond Iraq and Operation Iraqi Freedom. The primary research questions for this endeavor are: 1) What are the roots of sectarian violence? and 2) How will Islamic sectarianism influence or destabilize other legitimate governments in the Middle East?

According to the World English Dictionary, sectarian is defined as a member of a sect or faction, especially one who is bigoted in his adherence to its doctrines or in his intolerance toward other sects.[5] When members of a religion break into different sects, a core group is created, which is generally considered the advantaged group, and a minority group remains, which is generally considered the disadvantaged group. In its early history, Islam broke into the Sunni and the Shia sects.

This monograph will focus only on the major differences between the Sunni and Shia sects of Islam – in addition to these sects, there are many factions within each of these sects – and its scope will be limited to the Middle East. The Middle East is generally considered the land and sea contained in the nations from Egypt in the West to Afghanistan in the East and as far North as Kazakhstan and as far South as Yemen[6]. This monograph delimits the geographical area under study to the Middle East because the density of Shia outside of the Middle East is so small that conflict between sects rarely occurs.

American interests are deeply rooted in the Middle East and moving forward as we become more interconnected socially and economically, we will need to understand sectarian

---

5 Collins English Dictionary – Complete & Unabridged 10th Edition, "Sectarianism", Dictionary.Com, http://dictionary.reference.com/browse/Sectarianism (accessed November 18, 2010)

6 Arthur Goldschmidt Jr and Lawrence Davidson, *A Concise History of the Middle East*, Eighth Edition, (Boulder, CO.: Westview Press, 2005), 6.

cultural nuances in order to effectively conduct military operations there. The United States'

dependency on oil and natural resources in the Middle East creates economic ties as well. Our

interdependency with the Middle East will continue in the near future, as evidenced in an 13

April 2010 news conference by the President of the United States, Barack Obama; he stated that

the Middle East Dispute was "a vital national security interest of the United States."[7] When the

United States has a vital interest in an area, it focuses its elements of national power for the

purposes of maintaining access to the region. However as a military the United States lacks the

cultural understanding to be successful in the Middle East.

The United States' successful involvement in the Middle East requires a more culturally

astute Soldier, Sailor, Airman and Marine. Without a depth of cultural knowledge, our forces can

fall into traps constructed by cultural metaphors. Montgomery McFate is a leading scholar who

argues that deeper cultural understanding is necessary for successful warfare. In an article

McFate says that, "Marines were quick to acknowledge their misunderstanding of Iraqi culture [in

Operation Iraqi Freedom] particularly pertaining to physical culture and local symbols, and to

point out the consequences of inadequate training."[8]

One-example McFate details in her article directly addresses one of the cultural artifacts

of sectarianism in Iraq:

> In western tradition, a white flag means surrender. Many marines assumed a black flag
> was the opposite of surrender—"a big black flag means shoot here!" as one officer
> pointed out. As a result many Shia who traditionally fly black flags from their homes as
> a religious symbol were identified as the enemy and shot at unnecessarily[9]

---

7 Mark Landler and Helene Cooper, *"Obama Speech Signals a U.S. Shift on the Middle East"*, NY Times, 14 April 2010

8 McFate, Montgomery, *"The Military Utility of Understanding Adversary Culture"*, Joint Forces Quarterly, 38, (2005): 44

9 Ibid, 45

With proper cultural training, our military forces can make better tactical decisions on the battlefield. Had anyone in the formation cited above known that Shia fly black-flags to commemorate the suffering of Husayn,[10] it could have prevented unnecessary deaths, thereby providing a greater sense of security among the local population. However, at least one person in that formation needed to posses the depth of cultural knowledge required to inform the unit of the proper meaning of that symbol in context.

If you continue the cultural training required into higher levels of command, then knowledge begins to affect events occurring in both the tactical and the operational realms. The thesis of this monograph is that sectarian splits in the Muslim religion, particularly in the Middle East, offer western militaries operational and strategic opportunities that are currently not being explored.

Methodology

The methodology used to make the case for this monograph is the "most different" systems design described by Adam Przeworski and Henry Tuene. This methodology is "based on a set of cases as diverse as possible in which the analyst traces similar process of change."[11] This allows for a broad range of cases to be examined in order to find commonalities from which generalizations can be derived. When selecting cases to include as part of the methodology, it is important to find cases that share a dependant variable. Thus, when comparing the cases, all other divergences particular to a specific case becomes the independent variables. This monograph will explore sectarianism within Islam as the dependant variable.

---

10 Husayn ibn Ali was the second son of Ali ibn Abi Talib, the fourth Caliphate of Islam and the grandson of the Prophet Mohammed. He will killed in an ambush outside of Karbala in 680 AD.

11 Dankwart A. Rustow and Kenneth P. Erickson, *Comparative Political Dynamics: Global Research Perspectives* (New York, NY.: Harpercollins College Div, 1990), 17.

As Dr. David Rueda from Oxford University comments, Przeworski and Tuene's "most different" different systems is a variation of John Stuart Mills Method of Agreement[12]. Mills Method of Agreement states that if two or more instances of the phenomenon under investigation have only one circumstance in common, the circumstance in which alone all instances agrees, is the cause (or effect) of the given phenomenon.[13] Using these methodologies, this monograph will examine relationships within our cases and, in the analysis section, attempt to divine means that western militaries can use at the operational and strategic levels in the Middle East to pursue their diplomatic agendas.

This monograph will begin by explaining the historical context of the Sunni/Shia split. The historical examination contained herein will focus on the friction between the Sunni and Shia that began with Mohammed's death in 632 A.D., and continues today. The history of Islam and the Sunni/Shia split provided the impetus for the centuries of violence that followed. To illustrate this cycle of violence, this monograph will use two contemporary case studies.

The first case this monograph will explore is the al-Houthi rebellion in Yemen. A persecuted minority in Yemen the Shia al-Houthi fight for better treatment and recognition by the government of their unique culture that is threatened by the Sunni-dominated government in Sana'a. Although they are a minority in Yemen, the al-Houthi comprise the majority in several of the northern districts. This monograph will show the history of Yemen and the roots of the insurgency. It will detail the Yemeni government's response to the insurgency, and finally the ramifications of the insurgency in the region.

---

12 Reuda, David, "*How to Compare Countries Lecture 2*", Oxford University, http://webcache.googleusercontent.com/search?q=cache:xO1S8Yt86k4J:users.ox.ac.uk/~polf0050/Rueda%2520How%2520to%2520Compare%2520Countries%2520Lecture%25202.ppt+przeworski+most+different+systems&cd=2&hl=en&ct=clnk&gl=us , (Accessed November 21, 2010)

13 John Stuart Mill, *A System of Logic: Ratiocinative and Inductive*, 8th ed. (New York: Harper & Brothers Publishing, 1904), 280

The second case this monograph will explore is Syria. Predominantly Sunni Muslims populate Syria; however, a Shia minority governs it. This monograph will explain how the Shia came to power in Syria and it will explore the current democratic movements in the country. Additionally, it will determine what the ramifications of democracy would be on the ruling minority. Further, the monograph will explain the tensions placed on Syria from interstate actors, namely Saudi Arabia, Iran, and Iraq, which are all attempting to influence the country.

Finally, this monograph will provide recommendations that operational and strategic planners can utilize when analyzing our engagements in the Middle East thereby enhancing western opportunities there.

Literature Review: Conflict

The literature examined for this monograph will focus on conflict theories from the level of civilization down to sectarian violence. This chapter will step from broad wide-ranging conflict through ever narrowing and more specific types of conflict to arrive at a narrowly focused and personal level, sectarian conflict. The chapter begins with conflict between great civilizations and cultures and steps down from alliances to nations to tribal and finally ends with examining sectarian conflict. "Conflict" is really too broad of a term for this examination without additional modification being added. The portion of conflict theory that applies most closely to this research is the role of identity within conflict. Researchers have focused great effort on explaining the reasons for conflict and many of them offer predictive models for determining where conflict may next occur. This monograph will move beyond predictive analysis and into practical application of national power to gain advantages in conflicts that western nations may become involved with in the Middle East.

Civilizations

Broadly, civilizations divide the world in which we live. Samuel Huntington, a popular American political scientist, links the identity of culture to civilization. Huntington opines,

"Civilization identities are shaping the patterns of cohesion, disintegration, and conflict in the post-Cold War world."[14] His major contemporary civilizations are Sinic, (Chinese, Vietnamese, and Korean), Japanese, Hindu, Islamic, Orthodox, Western, Latin American, and possibly African.[15]

One of Huntington's main themes is that the "West won the world not by the superiority of its ideas or values or religion…but rather by its superiority in applying organized violence."[16] Here he begins to establish a thesis that the clash between civilizations is the root of violence, and that the West is the most prolific purveyor of violence in contemporary times. He further argues that in the post-Cold War world, states increasingly define their interests in civilizational terms and they ally themselves with similar cultures. These civilizations then engage in violent conflict with those outside of their civilization.[17]

Broadly, the argument is sound, but it over-simplifies other aspects of conflict. It is reductionist to the point of losing definition. The co-mingling of cultures in contemporary society occurs to such a degree that Huntington's categories are too broad. Moreover, Huntington's proscribed civilizations have unique aspects of cultural identity.

Cultural identity provides a link to continue to explore conflict. In their book, *Norms, Identity, and Culture in National Security*, authors Jepperson, Wendt, and Katzenstien put forth a persuasive argument about cultural identity in the use of power to establish national security. Jeppersons's argument refers to three layers of international cultural environments: formal institutions (alliances), world political culture (sovereignty and international law), and

---

[14] Samuel Huntington, *The Clash of Civilizations and the Remaking of World Order*, (New York: Simon and Schuster, 2003), 20

[15] Ibid., 45

[16] Ibid., 51

[17] Ibid., 34

international patterns of amity and enmity (historical friend/foe relationships).[18] This argument recognizes the role of civilization during conflict; however, the inclusion of the three layers broadens the lens when looking at other aspects of conflict and its origin. What is the role of these formal institutions in conflict, and what role do alliances play?

Alliances

Alliances are the natural extension of Huntington's theory of civilizations. If like-cultured civilizations work together for common goals, then formalizing those shared ideals through alliance structures establishes another identity level for conflict formation. One theory about alliances is that "States balance rather than bandwagon; alliances form because weak states band together against great powers in order to survive in an anarchic international system."[19] Further, Stephen Walt, a professor at Harvard University's John F. Kennedy School of Government, theorizes that states "balance threat," meaning that states align against what they perceive as threats rather than against economic and military capabilities.[20] This is consistent with one of the three layers in Jepperson's first argument (noted above) which states that international patterns of enmity are a primary motivator for building alliances.

Successful alliances form in what Karl Deutsch called a "pluralistic security community." This community shares many of the cultural ideologies in Huntington's civilization argument. Deustsch defines this community as "mutual sympathy and loyalties of 'we-feeling,' trust, and consideration."[21] He also argues that these occur in mostly democratic nations. In non-

---

[18] Peter J. Katzenstein, ed., *The Culture of National Security: Norms and Identity in World Politics (New Directions in World Politics)* (Chichester: Columbia University Press, 1996), 34.

[19] Thomas Risse-Kappen*, The Culture of National Security: Norms and Identity in World Politics; Collective Identity in a Democratic Community: The Case of Nato Edited by Peter J. Katzenstien,* (New York: Columbia University Press, 2009), 359.

[20] Ibid., 360

[21] Ibid., 368

democratic nations there is "nothing in their values that would prescribe mutual sympathy, trust, and consideration. Rather cooperation in non-democracies is likely to emerge out of narrowly defined self-interests."[22] These arguments apply to NATO and, more specifically, as Huntington would suggest, to Western civilization. Will the same hold true for an Arab alliance or Islamic civilization?

Islamic civilization is primarily centered in the Middle East. Applying Professor Walt's theory of balance of threat in this region shows an incompatibility to form alliances because of the "observation that Arab States, which supposedly share an identity, have quite a flair for conflict and not cooperation"[23] This supports Deustsch's argument regarding non-democracies.

Michael Barnett, professor at George Washington University's Elliot School of International Affiars, lends further credence to such an argument, citing that during an Arab League meeting after the Gulf War, "Arab states agreed for the first time that each could identify its own security threat. These testimonials suggest that the emergence of statist identities and the corresponding decline of Arab national identities enabled Arab leaders to assert that they no longer shared a definition of threat or should attempt to coordinate their security."[24] Clearly, this suggests that Arab countries are attempting to do their own "balance of force" as loosely coordinated, like-minded nations, and not as an alliance or a civilization.

National

In terms of identity, national identity is frequently the first affiliation that is applied to an individual in the international community. Moreover, national identity is the identity most often

---

[22] Ibid., 368

[23] Michael N. Barnett, , *The Culture of National Security: Norms and Identity in World Politics; Identity and Alliances in the Middle East, Edited by Peter J. Katzenstien*, (New York, Columbia University Press, 2009), 359

[24] Ibid., 429

explored by social scientists to explain behavior. In international relations, the two predominate paradigms or theories - realist and liberal - view the state as the primary actor in conflict. Since the advent of nation-states, national identity has created very strong connections for most people.

Anthony Smith, professor at London School of Economics, argues, "the appeal to national identity has become the main legitimation [sic.] for social order and solidarity today."[25] However, Smith also states that the formation of national identities created another layer of conflict. Nationalism is a narrow construct that is conflict laden because groups strive for legitimacy and it pits culture communities against one another. Moreover, because of the vast number of different culture communities, conflict becomes an eternal cycle.[26] Huntington limits the role of nations in conflict when he asserts, "[n]ation states are and will remain the most important actors in world affairs, but their interests, associations and conflicts are increasingly shaped by cultural and civilization factors."[27]

When taken together, these theorists suggest that two types of conflict can and must exist between nations. First, there are conflicts in which a state, singularly or, in conjunction with an alliance, has/have conflict with other states or non-state actors. Alternatively, a second type of conflict occurs when a state has conflict within its borders. Culture also plays a large role in conflict this theme is almost universal.

Huntington argues that there are no clear lines in civilizations and the borders between them blur on the edges.[28] Thus, on the borders of civilizations we find a propensity for conflict. Additionally, on the boundaries of cultural differences we also find a similar propensity for conflict. "Nationalism is based on the assumption that national identity groups want to create a

---

[25] Anothony D. Smith, *National Identity,*(London, Penguin Books, 2009), 16

[26] Ibid., 18

[27] Ibid., 36

[28] Huntington, 43

political unit, usually a state, in which to reside."[29] National identity is an amalgamation of many layers of other identities that include economic class, race, tribal/clan, or religion. Conflict exists in all of these aforementioned layers of national identity. However the in the study of sectarian conflict religion plays the central role.

Religion

Religion is one of the most important aspects of individual identity and a strong motivator of human behavior. Religion gives individuals a framework that allows them to see their place in the universe and helps them answer fundamental questions such as Who are we? Where do we come from? Why are we here? How should we behave?[30] Jonathan Fox, in his book, *Religion, Civilization, and Civil War,* critically examines Huntington's argument in *Clash of Civilizations* and determines that, "when comparing the impact of the two [civilization and religion], religion's impact is stronger more often than the impact of civilization."[31] Thus, when examining conflict, religion stands at the forefront as a cause of conflict.

Religion is one of the variables of culture and it is not constrained by national borders. Religion may become fragmented over time and sub-divided into sects that develop their own unique cultures. Sects of the main religion always begin as a minority and as such are subject to bigotry, discrimination, and hatred arising from the group dynamic. In the book, *Identity Matters* authors Peacock, Thorton, and Inman state that the term "sectarian" has a pejorative connotation and the term… "sectarian conflict" implies that if those involved in conflict would set aside their irrational attachments to their blood or fictive kin, and discard divisive, marginal religious attitudes, and adopt modern, live-and-let-live practices of tolerance… religious violence would

---

[29] Jonathan Fox, *Religion, Civilization, and Civil War: 1945 through the New Millennium* (Cambridge: Lexington Books, 2004), 17.

[30] Ibid., 18

[31] Ibid., 226

11

cease.[32] Sadly, those sectarian divides generally led to a dichotomy of the advantaged and disadvantaged.

In Islam when comparing the two major sects Sunni and Shia, the Shia are the predominantly disadvantaged community. Why should we focus on Islam? Huntington suggests, "Islamic civilization will be the most violent civilization and primary threat to the West in the post-cold war era."[33] Further, Fox's research supports Huntington's assertion in two ways. First, since 2000, Muslim ethnic groups have rebelled more frequently than other religious groups.[34] Second, since the mid-1970s those Muslim groups became the most violent of religious groups in conflict. [35] Thus when looking at ways to explore and exploit opportunities in the Middle East for creating advantages for western militaries sectarian identity provides the most advantageous place to begin.

History of the Sunni/Shia Split

The difference between Sunni and Shia began with a difference in perception in the succession of leadership within Islam. Over time, that perception grew into differences in practice of their faith. This chapter will briefly describe the history of the Sunni/Shia divide. Because each sect has a different perspective on Islam, the practices of the two sects diverged over time and that divergence is the root cause of the cycle of sectarian violence. The differences spring forth from political origins. On June 8, 632 C.E., the prophet Muhammad passed from this world into the next. Before he died, he did not identify a successor to his newly formed religion and government. The title by which the Islamic sects identify themselves shows how the conflict begins.

---

[32] James L. Peacock, Patricia M. Thornton, and Patrick B. Inman, *Identity Matters: Clues to Understand Ethnic and Sectarian Conflict*, (New York: Berghahn Books, 2007), 212

[33] Jonathan Fox, *Religion, Civilization, and Civil War: 1945 through the New Millennium*, 168

[34] Ibid., 47

[35] Ibid., 55

The term Sunni is derived from the term *Sunna,* the Arabic term for tradition. As tradition would have dictated in 632 C.E. in the tribal areas of Arabia, major decisions affecting the tribe would have been made by a *Shura*-- an "intertribal forum where agreements were ratified and disputes were settled."[36] Muhammad said, "My community will never agree in error."[37] Thus, it was natural for the Sunni to believe that a quorum of intertribal leaders would determine the next patriarch for the *ummah,* the name for the growing community of Islamic believers. Upon conclusion of the *Shura* , the first Caliph (Commander of the Faithful) of the Muslims, Abu Bakr, was selected.

Muhammad had ten wives during his life. His first wife Khadija, birthed four daughters and two sons. The sons did not live past infancy, and his beloved wife died while his daughters were still young. He married his next wives in an effort to strengthen his grip on the growing empire. His favorite of the new wives was Aisha, the daughter of Abu Bakr. Abu Bakr was one of Muhammad's original partners who stood by him as Muhammad began to reveal the words of God passed through the Angel Gabriel. As such, the S*hura* determined, the mantle of leadership passed to the father-in-law of the prophet.

However, not all of Islam belived that was the proper succession of the mantle of leadership. The term Shia means party in Arabic. It is a shortening of the phrase *Shi'at Ali* or party of Ali.[38] Ali, the Shia believe, should have been the first Caliph and the succession should have passed down through the bloodline of Muhammad, via the Arabic principle of *nasb,* or royal bloodlines.

---

[36] Lesley Hazleton, *After the Prophet: The Epic Story of the Shia-Sunni Split in Islam* (New York: Anchor, 2010), 58.

[37] Ibid., 61

[38] Graham E. Fuller and Rend Rahim Francke, *The Arab Shi'a: The Forgotten Muslims* (New York: Palgrave Macmillan, 2001), 6.

Who was Ali and why did he claim the rightful leadership over Abu Bakr, the father of Muhammad's favorite wife? Ali was Muhammad's earliest companion, his paternal cousin and the first convert to Islam.[39] So beloved was Ali that Muhammad gave his eldest daughter Fatima to him in marriage, above many other suitors and potential allies.[40] Ali and Fatima gave Muhammad that which he did not have on his own two male children, Hasan and Hussein. Together Muhammad, his four daughters, son-in-law and two grandsons were the *Ahl al-Bayt,* the people of the family of the prophet.[41]

On 10 March 632 on his return from his final pilgrimage to Mecca, at an oasis named Ghadir Khumm, Shia scholars claim that Muhammad made this declaration:

> The time approaches when I shall be called away by God and I shall answer that call. I am leaving you with two precious things and if you adhere to both of them, you will never go astray. They are the Quran, the book of God, and my family, the People of the House, *Ahl al-Bayt.* They shall never separate from each other until they come to me by the pool of Paradise.[42]

Sunni scholars dispute the accuracy of this quote, however, considering that if Abu Bakr's claim was strong enough for him become Caliph, was not Ali's at least equally strong? Sadly, for history, Muhammad neither had a male heir nor was his son-in-law in attendance at the S*hura* that determined the passing of leadership in the emerging Islamic civilization. Ali was instead preparing Muhammad for burial in accordance with the direction of the faith. By the time Muhammad was properly cared for and sent to Paradise, the decision has been made and Ali did not contest it. The next 30 years Ali called his "years of dust and thorns."[43]

These decades marked the transition from the first to the fourth Caliph. Abu Bakr, the first Caliph, appointed Omar as the second Caliph. An assassin killed Omar and a Shura elected

---

[39] Lesley Hazleton, *After the Prophet: The Epic Story of the Shia-Sunni Split in Islam,* 36.

[40] Ibid, 37

[41] Graham E. Fuller and Rend Rahim Francke, *The Arab Shi'a: The Forgotten Muslims,* 13.

[42] Lesley Hazleton, *After the Prophet: The Epic Story of the Shia-Sunni Split in Islam,* 51.

[43] Ibid, 66

Othman over Ali as the third Caliph. This was done as a stopgap measure in order to be better positioned for the *Shura's* that would follow Othman's death. Othman, who came from the wealthy Umayyad tribe, proved to be a very poor Caliph and rather than living piously and humbly, began to covet the wealth that came with an expanding empire. Othman was murdered for his behavior and Ali took over the mantle of leadership of Islam on 16 June 656 C.E.

Ali rejected the term Caliph, Commander of the Faithful, which he felt the Umayyad's had tarnished beyond repair, and instead he would be known as *Imam*, he who stands in front.[44] Ali's reign as he who stands in front would last only five short years. Sunni refer to the first four Caliph as the *rashidun* or rightly guided ones, as each of the first four were among Muhammads first companions and converts to Islam. However, Sunni and Shia only agree on two of the first five leaders of Islam, Muhammad and Ali. The Shia call the first three Caliph's usurpers.[45]

At this point in history there is no difference between the Muslims. However, the perception is building in the differences between those who believe in the *Sunna* tradition of selecting leaders, and those who want the *Ahl al-Bayt* to become successive leaders. The Shia celebrates Ali as the first of 12 Imams, his successive heirs, and along with Fatima, as the *Ahl al-Bayt*. After Ali, the *Ahl al-Bayt* would never lead Islam again, and the Imams would only be leaders of a small but growing number of Shia.

Aisha, Muhammad's favorite wife at the time of his death, and who was known as Mother of the Faithful, raised an Army to defeat Ali. Aisha believed Ali had no claim as Caliph based on the long-standing feud between the two of them. Muslims killing Muslims was declared haram or forbidden by Muhammad. Thus, it was with great reluctance that Ali fought what was known as the Battle of the Camel, the first major Sunni/Shia sectarian fight. The followers of Ali

---

[44] Ibid, 100

[45] Heinz Halm and Allison Brown, *Shi'a Islam: From Religion to Revolution (Princeton Series on the Middle East)* (Princeton, NJ.: Markus Wiener Publishers, 1996), 5.

accepted his claim as Imam against the followers of Aisha, Mother of the Faithful, who claimed that Ali had killed Othman. The followers of Aisha believed that Ali had drawn Muslim blood first and as such, the battle was declared *halal* or sanctioned.

In 656 C.E. a *fitna* occurred. In Arabic, fitna is, "a terrible wrenching apart of the fabric of society, the unraveling of the tightly woven matrix of kinship, it is... the ultimate threat to Islam."[46] A prophecy attributed to a soldier from Basra stated, "This will lead to worse than what you most hate, it is a tear that will not be mended, a fracture that will never be repaired."[47] By midday, more than 3000 Muslims lay slain, most of them from Aisha's defeated Army. Aisha returned to Mecca, leaving Ali on the field.

Ali had no respite. While he was preparing for battle, Marwan, Othman's former deputy, took Othman's bloody shirt to Damascus. Here the governor of Syria, Muawiya, ordered the bloody shirt displayed in a mosque. Muawiya, another Umayyad, used this action as propaganda to forward his personal claim to Caliph. "Mu-a-wi-ya seemed almost tailor made for the Shia curses that would be heaped on the sect for centuries to come."[48]

The assassin who killed Ali with a poisoned sword was sent by Muawiya to cement his position as Caliph. Those who supported Ali's claim became *Shi'at Ali* and those who supported the claim of Muawiya became the Sunni. Ali's eldest son Hasan, the second Shia Imam, was indecisive and hesitant after his father's death and rather than fight to become Caliph, Hasan abdicated to Muawiya in Kufa, Iraq. Hasan passed away between 670-680 C.E. and Muawiya passed in 680 C.E. Muawiya designated his son Yazid the successor to Caliph ushering the era of *nasb*, the passing of Caliph by bloodlines, not as the Shia wanted to the *Ahl al-Bay*.

---

[46] Lesley Hazleton, *After the Prophet: The Epic Story of the Shia-Sunni Split in Islam*,108.

[47] Ibid, 110

[48] Ibid, 126

Hussein was Muhammad's closest living relation at this time. Shia supporters encouraged Hussein to come to Iraq and claim his rightful position as Imam. Muawiya knew this would occur and his last instructions to Yazid were, "If you defeat Hussein, pardon him, for he has a great claim."[49] Yazid did not heed the warnings of his politically astute father. Instead his minions brutally murdered Hussein, desecrated his body, and humiliated the other members of Muhammad's family on 10 October 680 outside of Karbala, Iraq. The Shia celebrate the martyrdom of Hussein at a reenactment of the massacre during, *Ashaura*, a ceremony that allows the Shia to fully vent their grief, remorse, and lamentation.[50] The two most important survivors of the Karbala massacre were Ali, the younger, and Zaynab, Hussein's sister and the granddaughter of Muhammad. Zaynab and Ali marched from Karbala to Damascus to confront Yazid whereupon Zaynab bereated Yazid. "You, your father, and your grandfather submitted to the faith of my father, Ali, the faith of my brother Hussein, the faith of my grandfather Muhammad...Yet you have vilified them unjustly and oppressed the very faith you profess."[51] Only fifty years after Muhammad's death, the men of his family had been massacred and the women humiliated. As the shame of these events spread throughout the Middle East, Muhammad's family took a new name, *Bayt al-Ahzan*, the house of sorrow.[52]

Ali the younger, the sole male survivor of Muhammad's lineage, became the fourth Imam and the lineage continued through him extending from his father in 656 C.E., the first Shia Imam and fourth Sunni Caliph, to the occultation of the 12th Imam in 873, Muhammad al-Mahdi, The Hidden Imam. Shia who accept the twelve Imams are called Twelver Shia and are the majority. The Hidden Imam was never seen in public and when his father, the 11th Imam died, there was a

---

[49] Ibid., 196.

[50] Graham E. Fuller and Rend Rahim Francke, *The Arab Shi'a: The Forgotten Muslims*, 13.

[51] Lesley Hazleton, *After the Prophet: The Epic Story of the Shia-Sunni Split in Islam*,196.

[52] Ibid., 192

major splintering of the Shia during a time the Sunni call *hayra,* or confusion.[53] Kufa, Iraq is the birthplace of both political and religious Shia Islam, and Iraq is where six of the twelve Imams are laid to rest.[54]

Shia'ism is often attributed as an Iranian phenomenon that is Persian in nature and thus foreign to Arabs.[55] Persia did not fully embrace Shia'ism until the sixteenth century and because of that many Iranian traditions found their way into the practice of the Shia faith. Moreover, that faulty image of Shia'ism emanating from Iran was reinforced by the Islamic revolution that occurred in 1979 and established Iran as a Shia theocracy. "In geographic sense, Shia'ism is on the peripheries of the Arab world, but in another sense it lies in the absolute heart of the Persian Gulf with its communities clustered around the old-rich shores of eastern Saudi Arabia, Bahrain, southern Iraq, Kuwait, and to a lesser extent, the United Arab Emirates, Qatar, Oman, and Yemen."[56] This places the Shia in one of the wealthiest areas on earth, although as a sect, they are repressed and under represented.

Sunni are the overwhelming majority of the worlds 1.3 billion Muslims. The Shia represents approximately 130-195 million people or 10-15 percent of total Muslims. In the Middle East from Lebanon to Pakistan, the Shia represents 50 percent of the Muslim population. However, in the Gulf Rim, they comprise more than 80 percent of the total population.[57] These are the regions of the world with the richest known deposits of fossil fuels. Previously, this area would have been considered "Arab" but as the identity shifts is not always true. In our contemporary environment more elements of identity must be considered when labeling

---

[53] Heinz Halm and Allison Brown, *Shi'a Islam: From Religion to Revolution,* 29.

[54] Ibid, 17

[55] Ibid, 17

[56] Graham E. Fuller and Rend Rahim Francke, *The Arab Shi'a: The Forgotten Muslims,* 18.

[57] Vali Nasr, *The Shia Revival: How Conflicts within Islam Will Shape the Future* (New York: W. W. Norton, 2006), 34.

geographic locations. This monograph will show that further understanding of identity will allow for increasing leverage by western governments and militaries influencing these sectarian rifts.

Case Study: Yemen

The Romans considered Yemen a land of plenty, and referred to Yemen as *Arabia Felix* - happy or prosperous Arabia. Yemen produced frankincense and myrrh, which are resins from the dried sap of local tress and were highly valuable commodities in ancient times. [58] Much of Arabia is dry sandy or rocky desert with the exception of Oman and Yemen. Here, moist air from the Indian Ocean and mountain springs combine to enable these areas to produce more agriculture and grow the trees that produce the valuable resin. [59] The availability of water and commerce "Supported the rise of more highly developed forms of political organizations than the rest of Arabia."[60] Muhammad had consolidated his power from Yathrib (Medina) to Mecca, and Yemen was the next likely place for the expansion of Islam.

Prior to the coming of Muhammad and Islam, a couple of distinct Jewish and Christian Kingdoms existed. These kingdoms were primarily tribal societies. King Dhu Nuwas of the Himyarites influenced the Yemeni Jewish tribes, which had bloody clashes with Christians. Great King Khorso II sent an expeditionary force from the Byzantine Empire to ensure access to the Indian Ocean and the Silk Road.[61] This long and bloody conflict set the stage for the expansion of Islam.

According to Islamic history, Ali brought Yemen into Islam. Ali's influence allowed the Muslim Army to capture Mecca without a fight. Also, Ali's repeated bravery in battle prompted

---

[58] Patrick Brogan, *World Conflicts: A Comprehensive Guide to World Strife Since 1945*, 3 Sub ed. (Lanham, Md.: The Scarecrow Press, Inc., 1999), 374.

[59] Fred M. Donner, *Muhammad and the Believers: At the Origins of Islam* (Cambridge: Belknap Press of Harvard University Press, 2010), 27.

[60] Ibid., 28.

[61] Ibid., 34.

Muhammad to send Ali to Yemen, and it is claimed that, "When he [Ali] was sent to Yemen he brought the whole country into the fold of Islam by his sermons."[62] This influence of Ali allowed the Growth of Shia'ism in Yemen beginning in 9th Century.

In 893 Yahya bin al-Husyan was invited to Yemen to mediate between fighting tribes in the northern highlands.[63] Yahya was a Shia Muslim, but of a specific sect called Zaydis. His mediation was successful and Yahya stayed in the region establishing a succession of Zaydi imamates from 893 to 1962.[64] The factional split from traditional Twelever Shia and Zayid's, sometimes called Fiver Shia by Sunni, occurred during the reign of the fifth Imam.

Zayd bin Ali is the great-grandson of the first Imam Ali, and therefore a direct descendant of the Prophet Muhammad. In 740 the Shi'at 'Ali, party of Ali staged a rebellion against the Umayyad Caliphate. Zayd bin 'Ali was killed leading that raid. Zaydi Shia believe that Zayd bin 'Ali was the fifth Imam. However, the Twelver Shia believes that Zayd's Brother Muhammad al-Baqir was the fifth Imam.[65]

As a result of this dissension the Zaydi's or Fiver Shia are born. The doctrine of Zaydism is a philosophy of rationalization where the Imam is the conduit of God's wisdom. By contrast, a Twelver is more of a textual literalist who believes that the Imam is infallible.[66] This difference allowed the Sunni and Shia communities to cohabitate more easily in Yemen because the "Zaydi Imamates demonstrated tolerance for Shafi'is, the dominant Sunni School of thought, in

---

[62] Islamic Occasions, "Second Infallible Ali (AS) the First Imam", Islamic Occasions: Truth Wisdom and Justice. http://www.ezsoftech.com/islamic/infallible2a.asp, (accessed December 21, 2101)

[63] Barak A. Salmoni, Bryce Loidolt and Madeleine Wells, *Regime and Periphery in Northern Yemen: The Huthi Phenomenon* (Santa Monica, CA.: Rand Publishing, 2010), 64.

[64] Ibid., 65

[65] Ibid., 64

[66] Ibid., 64

Yemen."[67] The Shia Imamates ruled Northern Yemen in an unbroken line of *sayyids,* desendants of the Prophet, via the joining of Ali and Fatima, until the 1960s.

The Imamates were not the only leadership that influenced the political landscape of Yemen. Many empires lay claim to Yemen - the Byzantines, the Caliphates, the Egyptians, and most recently, the English. The British captured the port of Aden in 1839 and expanded its influence into southern and eastern Yemen. British influence in Yemen continued from that point until 1965, when "most of the tribal states within the protectorates and the Aden colony proper had joined to form the British-sponsored Federation of South Arabia."[68]

However, as with many cases of British colonial rule, "The British imposed a wholly artificial division between North and South Yemen, in order to exert some control over Aden's hinterland."[69] These arbitrary lines drawn by a colonial power and the tribal divisions created were the cause of many deaths and the civil strife that followed as Yemen tried to unify. North Yemen, which became known as the Yemen Arab Republic (YAR), and South Yemen separately faced various struggles until the country was unified and they began working together.

Even though the Northern and Southern Yemini were working together, the Imamates still ruled the YAR. Trouble began upon the assassination of the Imamate Yahya in a coup attempt; however, Yahya's son Ahmad put down the coup.[70] Ahmad's rule in North Yemen focused on greater openness and tolerance and he aligned with the British and Egyptians to vex the British. Many Northern Yemeni men learned martial tactics from the Egyptians and when Ahmad died as an old man those military aged men and Egypt attempted a coup to wrest control of North Yemen from Ahmad succssor. Egypt quickly flew forces into Yemen on 26 September

---

[67] Ibid., 64

[68] Yemen Youngblood-Coleman, Denise, editor. *Country Review: Yemen. 2010.* Houston, Texas: CountryWatch Publications, 2010. Country Review:Yemen. Online. Available URL: http://www.countrywatch.com/cw_country.aspx?vcountry=188, accessed October, 12, 2010., 7

[69] Patrick Brogan, *World Conflicts: A Comprehensive Guide to World Strife Since 1945,* 374.

[70] Ibid., 375.

1962. Ahmad's son with support from the tribal Sheiks, Saudi Arabia and the British, routed the Egyptians within a month and stopped their encroachment on the Arabian Peninsula.[71]

The British were not having much success in Southern Yemen. In an effort to retain some semblance of control, Britain set up the "Federation of South Arabia, to be dominated by conservative sheikhs from the back country, in hope of leaving a pro-British government behind them, but radicals easily defeated them."[72] By 1967, the British had fled Yemen and the Soviet Union moved in to fill the void. South Yemen became the People's Democratic Republic of Yemen and the only communist state in the world with a state religion, Islam.[73]

The period of post-colonial rule saw numerous assassinations in both North and South Yemen. South Yemen evicted its Soviet Rulers in 1986, and that eventually led to the re-unification the two Yemens into a single country on 22 May 1990. Unfortunately, the re-unification did not end Yemen's internal strife.

Two factors from re-unification played an important role in the Al-Houthi rebellion. First, prior to re-unification a secular government was established in the North, which had lost its connection with the historical rule of the *al-byat*, the house of the family. Second, "The estimation of the percentage of Sunni's in Yemen range from 50%-55% … [which] dominated the south and Red Sea Coast."[74] These factors set the stage for an insurgency to grow in the northern governance of Sa'da. The Southern tribes had access to the port of Aden, which was modernized by both the British and the Soviets and brought wealth to the southern tribes and access to the government ruling from Sana'a.

---

[71] Ibid., 374.

[72] Ibid., 375.

[73] Ibid., 376.

[74] Barak A. Salmoni, Bryce Loidolt and Madeleine Wells, *Regime and Periphery in Northern Yemen: The Huthi Phenomenon* ,73.

The government in Sana'a was not effective at recognizing this insurgency in the beginning, and it has not been overly effective in quelling it. This has led to an overall lawlessness in modern Yemen. The rise of the rebellion did not happen quickly nor was it caused by a single factor. The Houthi's primary seat of power in Sa'da did not see the arrival of the YAR until 1969 and most northern areas didn't receive representatives from the Government of Yemen (GoY) until 1980s.[75] In 1979, the GoY built a paved road between the Capitol Sana'a and the Sa'da the capitol of the governance with the same name. The road reduced the travel time between the two cities from 10 hours to 4 hours and allowed more varied types of vehicles to make the trip.[76]

One result of opening the Yemeni North was that people of varying social strata were exposed to one another and individuals started to see the differences in wealth and possessions. The northern tribal Sheikhs began to see the difference in wealth between themselves and the Southern Sheikhs. Moreover, a mixing of the tribes began to occur between the *qabili* (tribal person) and the non-*qabili*, and between the Hashimis (tribal descendants of Muhammad) and the non-*sayyid* Zaydis.[77] This tribal mixing diminished the value of being related to Muhammad and having the Shia recognized authority to rule.

The GoY was leery of the influence of the Northern tribes and their historical roots to the Imamates and took measures to reduce the influence of the Northern Sheikhs. The GoY, in an effort to stabilize its control of Yemen, began to give money and access to younger *qabili* in the form of government grants to buy pumps for wells, educational opportunities, seedlings, and money.[78] The rise in the status and wealth of the younger generation brought the tribal Sheikhs

---

[75] Ibid., 81.

[76] Ibid., 81.

[77] Ibid., 84.

[78] Ibid., 87.

closer to the government. In turn, the Sheikhs learned from the government how to buy land and acquire it from the members of their tribes thereby increasing their power. The ramifications of these actions created a gulf between the Sheikhs and their tribe members. It separated the tribe members from the land, which is an important tribal value. As a result, tribal members concluded that the Sheikhs were more "concerned with farms and government connections than about the tribal value."[79] This began to erode the influence of the Sheikhs and prevented them from being able to fulfill their role as arbitrators and mediators because of their perceived lack of impartiality.

The Sunni influence also affected the roots of the rebellion. As one of the most impoverished countries in the Middle East, Yemini workers would leave the country to seek work and send money home to their families. In 1990, Iraq invaded Kuwait and the newly re-unified Yemeni government did not support Saudi Arabia's invitation to the United States to expel the Iraqis from Kuwait. The Saudi's interpreted this stance as implicit support from Yemen to Iraq and the consequence was the Saudi government ejecting one million Yemeni workers back to their homes. In Sa'da from 1975-1994 the population had quadrupled and the returning workers found more competition for land and commercial markets.[80] Economics competition, however, was far from the worst effect that the repatriation caused.

While the Yemeni expatriates were working in Saudi Arabia, they were exposed to the same Salafism thinking that the *mujahidin* (freedom fighters) in Afgahinstan were and they found it appealing.[81] This is the basis of *Wahhabism*, the brand of Islam practiced by al-Qaeda, which

---

[79] Ibid., 85.

[80] Ibid., 88.

[81] Ibid., 89.

is based on the teachings of Muhammad ibn Abdul-Wahhab (1703-1792). The terms Wahhabism and Salafism are used interchangeably when addressing this specific practice of Islam.[82]

In Salafism, the main teaching is the "intellectual tradition of *Tawhid,* which is focused on the oneness of God as understood through direct encounter with the Qur'an unmediated by centuries of scholarly commentaries or worldly accommodations…focused on the equality of all Muslims, considering the excessive veneration of 'Ali and his descendants as a derogation of monotheism."[83] Wahhibism Islam is taught in *Madrasa's* (schools of theological learning) mosques and study circles. Wahhibism Islam is also described in pamphlets that are circulated all over Saudi Arabia and are exported around the world. The Saudi Madrasa's created a new generation of learned Yemeni men and when these men returned to Yemen they brought the Salafism teaching and techniques with them.

When Saudi Arabia expelled the Yemeni workers, they returned to Yemen with their new beliefs and received support in these teachings from the GoY. The leaders of a newly unified Yemen viewed this incursion of Salafism as a hedge against the southern separatists and the Zaydi elites. The al-Houthi tribal leaders recognized these two major threats to their identity and responded by creating a parallel structure to reinforce their historical religious teachings and reestablish the tribal elder's role as leader and Sheppard. This parallel structure of schools, outreach programs, religious centers, public support, and youth camps became the Believing Youth.[84] Additionally, this was an impetus to create a new political party, the al-Haqq, to counter what S*ayyid* Ahmed bin Muhammad bin 'Ali al-Shami, the party's general secretary, stated regarding Wahhabism:

---

[82] Sunna.org, "http://www.sunnah.org/articles/Wahhabiarticleedit htm", by Zubair Qamar, accessed on 07 Feb 2011.

[83] Barak A. Salmoni, Bryce Loidolt and Madeleine Wells, *Regime and Periphery in Northern Yemen: The Huthi Phenomenon,* 89.

[84] Ibid., 90

Wahhabism is a child of imperialism…we are seeing imperialism in our country in its Islamic guise…Saudi Arabia is pouring lots and lots of money into Yemen to promote its own version of Wahhabi Islam…So, we need to counter these efforts.[85]

The combination of youth outreach and political activism became a growing threat to the leadership in Sa'ana. Thus, the friction points were established. Confrontation between the GoY and the al-Houthi are a by-product of losing a sense of identity on one side and the government trying to maintain tenuous control over a newly formed country on the other.

Historical, social, and political roots all run through the rebellion. Another unfortunate consequence of the al-Houthi view and distrust of the government is the view the Shia took regarding the Yemeni Government and United States relations. Post 9-11, the US began seeking partners in the Global War on Terror and found a willing ally in Yemen. The Houthi took to describing the relationship between the Government of Yemen and the Government of the United States as one wherein the GoY is an agent or 'amil of the US.

The historical hatred of Islam against Judaism combined with the support the US gives to Israel created a logic loop by the Houthi – Muslims hate Jews, the US loves Jews, President Sahl'ah and the GoY love the US, thus we hate the government. The al-Houthi motto chanted at the end of the Friday sermons is, "al-Mawt li Amrika al-Mawt li Isra'il al-La'na 'ala-l-Yahud, al-Nasr li-l-Islam; Death to America, Death to Israel, Curse upon the Jews, Victory for Islam!"[86] With any approach where western powers attempt to influence Yemen, this view must be countered. One of the ways western countries have tried to destroy this cultural friction is in military-to-military cooperation in Yemen.

Western militaries are already engaged in Yemen as advisors assisting in training the Yemeni Special Forces. In a recent 60 Minutes Special Steve Kroft reported on the training that is taking place between Western and Yemeni forces. Kroft reported, "Officially, the only US

---

[85] Ibid., 95

[86] Ibid., 119

military presence in Yemen is a contingent of about 50 trainers working with Yemen's counterterrorism forces."[87] Moreover, he asserts, "the government's official position is that the US can't be involved militarily there and needs to let the Yemenis take on al-Qaeda...but there is no question that US military involvement goes far beyond the 50 trainers."[88] This is exactly where the Western militaries must engage in order to be operationally effective in Yemen because this access allows greater leverage in effecting change in the region.

Operationally the West has specific opportunities to effect change in Yemen. The military advisors who reside in Yemen today must take steps to assist the religious rift in Yemen and get the government and the al-Houthi to repair their relationship. These advisors operate at the operational level and provide a bottom up effect in the formation and implementation of policy. The importance of this alliance is in the best interest of western governments and militaries. Al-Qaeda has said openly that it opposes and will kill the Zaydis because they are apostates. This tension can be leveraged by western forces.

This leverage is possible because of the historical context. Aposteses is the worst crime that a Muslim can commit. Turning one's back on Allah and not worshiping Islam is punishable by death. This is the rationale behind why there is so much Islamic sectarian violence. The wahhibbists driving the sectarian wedge in the country of Yemen is the fulcum to exploit.

US and UK advisors must, through their military contacts, advise their counterparts on how to best repair the relationship between the government and the al-Houthi tribesmen. By drawing upon their knowledge of the history of Islam in Yemen these advisors, who possess high-level government access can effect these changes. Subtle suggestions made from a position of knowledge, combined with an understanding of both the historical context and the current

---

[87] http://ebird.osd.mil/ebfiles/e20110117800462.html, Early Bird, 60 Minutes transcript Aired January 16, 2011, accessed January 18, 2011

[88] Ibid.

situation will have the greatest affect when attempting to change the direction of the government. A way to accomplish this difficult task is using amnesty, reconciliation, and reintegration, AR2 theory. This process is described by Michael Mosser, assistant professor at the United States Army's Command and General Staff College, in his article *The "Armed Reconciler."* The military advisors can use this process to influence the Yemini Government. Once the government offers amnesty to the al-Houthi and begins the reconciliation and reintegration process it will strengthen the country.

Once the country is more stable and the government is more secure from internal threats, then the advisors can help shape the engagement between the government and the al-Qaeda threat. With the assistance of the northern Zaydi tribes and the government, the ability to gather intelligence and begin to both develop and track high-value targets in the country of Yemen is expanded. Developing key allies against violent extremist organizations is important and in the borders of Yemen is critical. The ability to turn the Yemeni Shia against an organization that threatened their existence should not be that difficult. These small operational steps can make great strides in making Yemen a more stable country and reducing the international threat that emanates from its lawless regions. Western militaries can affect greater change in this region for the benefit of the world.

Case Study: Syria

In 2500 B.C.E., the city of Damascus, the oldest continuously inhabited capitol city in the world, was founded.[89] "Syria was occupied successively by Canaanites, Phoenicians, Hebrews, Arameans, Assyrians, Babylonians, Persians, Greeks, Romans, Nabateans, Byzantines

---

[89] Youngblood-Coleman, Denise, editor. *Country Review: Syria. 2010*. Houston, Texas: CountryWatch Publications, 2010. Country Review:Syria. Online. Available URL: http://www.countrywatch.com/cw_country.aspx?vcountry=167, accessed October, 12, 2010., 7

and, in part, Crusaders, before coming under the control of the Ottoman Turks."[90] Damascus or Syria has always played a role as a central actor in Middle Eastern politics and religion. In additional, to the aforementioned list rulers of modern Syria, one must also include the Mongols, British, and French who also played major roles in shaping Syria as it exists today. At one point, however, Damascus did know a period of great power and influence.

The Damascan height of power and influence occurred in 636 C.E. when it became the home of the Islamic Caliphate. After Muawiya assassinated Ali, he established the Umayyad dynasty in Damascus. Muawiya built much of what became the governing aspects of Islam and although the city where the Caliphate would come to rest changed throughout history, it began in Damascus. From 661 C.E. to 750 C.E., Damascus was the capitol of the Omayyad Empire that controlled territory from Spain to Africa across the Middle East and Central Asia to India. Sunni Muslims controlled this broad swath of land and its people. In contrast, modern Syria is controlled and governed by a minority Shia sect known as Alawi, or sometimes referred to as the Nusayris.

The Alawi came to power over a long and circuitous route. Matti Moosa, author of *Extremist Shiite,s* characterized Shias in the following manner, "the extremist of these sects is essentially religious, and should not be confused with the religio-political radicalism of the Shiite regime in Iran and its antagonism of the West. The extremist Shiites discussed in this book are peaceful people, and, except for the Nusayris of Syria they do not seem to be political activists or to have assumed political power."[91] How is it that in this hotbed of sectarianism a hated and feared minority came to power? The name Alawi, which the Nusaryians preferred to be called,

---

[90] Ibid., 7

[91] Matti Moosa, *Extremist Shiites: The Ghulat Sects (Contemporary Issues in the Middle East)* (Syracuse: Syracuse University Press, 1988), ix.

means followers or Ali.[92] The Alawi tribes, like Ali, are survivors and waited patiently over the course of many generations for an opportunity to take power.

That the Alawi survived for so long as a persecuted minority was due in large part to their geographic location. The existence of the Nusayruyya Mountains which stretch from north to south along the western fringe of the country, allowed the Alawi to escape and hide from their persecutors and flourish within certain parameters. The Nusaryians developed a unique cultural and religious identity. The Nusaryians hated the Sunni and the Christians and acted on that hatred by, "taking revenge on the Muslim people of the plains… plundering and killing without mercy."[93] Their predilection for violence reduced them to "a state of barbarism and left the country a wasteland, violence, bloodshed, treachery, and murder became a way of life with the Nusayris."[94] The devastation wrought on the Nusaryian communities forced them to move closer to the urban areas and change their identity they became known as hardworking and subservient and no threat to their employers' interests.[95] Moreover, the Muslim and Christian landowners needed the services of the Nusayris farmers. Over time, the hated and persecuted Shia minority became an invaluable section of society without which Syrian society could not function, for it was the working class of Shia who provided food stores to the majority Sunni.

Like other persecuted religious minorities in closed societies, the Alawi "acquired what may be called an inferiority complex, regarding themselves as forlorn and despised people. Yet… they claimed to be a "chosen people"[96] The Alawi lived in constant fear of the "Sunnite Wolf" that is the Arab Sunnite government in Damascus."[97] Through the ages the Alawi were constantly

---

[92] Ibid., 255.

[93] Ibid., 257.

[94] Ibid., 257.

[95] Ibid., 257.

[96] Ibid., 269

[97] Ibid., 285

persecuted at the hands of the Arab Sunni, the Mongols, the Crusaders, and the Ottomans. The fall of the Ottoman Empire combined with the introduction of European influence finally brought the opportunity for self-governance to the Alawi.

During a trip to Damascus in 1916 Faysal ibn al Husyan, the leader of Syria at the time, was drawn into a secret society called the Al-Fatat whose goal was the liberation of all Arab land from European and Turkish control. The British bargained with the Arabs and agreed to support their bid for independence. It was agreed that, "they [the British] should create an independent state that would include the Arab lands of the Middle East."[98] However, the British also entered into contradictory pacts with other European powers and once the war was over decided to, "honor those with their fellow Europeans: the French and the Zionists."[99] The Arabs never forgave this betrayal. Moreover, governance of Syria passed to the French. There was a great deal of machinations by the French in Syria during the interwar period, but World War II settled the entire affair and Syria became an independent nation on 17 April 1946.

As with many Middle Eastern countries, the establishment of a sovereign nation did not usher in an era of peace and tranquility, but instead began a series of violent upheavals over a period of decades to establish a recognized "normalcy." The political landscape of the Middle East post-World War II was very turbulent. How does a minority group that was persecuted for centuries take charge of the government under the noses of its tormentors? The Alawis' rise to power was a slow and deliberate process that occurred via two means "the Army and the Baath Party."[100] These two entities were instrumental in helping to make the transition from colonial rule to self-rule. As with all transitions of power, elements of luck and skill are also involved. The Alawi worked diligently from the bottom up in these organizations to take them over.

---

[98] Arthur Goldschmidt Jr and Lawrence Davidson, *A Concise History of the Middle East*, 214.

[99] Ibid., 214

[100] Matti Moosa, *Extremist Shiites: The Ghulat Sects*, 292.

The French began raising an Army when they realized that they would not be capable of ruling indefinitely in the region. Joining this Army was not that appealing to the majority of Syrians, but because life was so hard for some minority Nusayrians they felt forces to enlist their sons into the Army. "In the mountain regions families were forced to sell their daughters to wealthy townspeople as domestic servants because they could not support them at home."[101]

Being in the Army furthered a soldier's education and, as in many cultures, sons followed fathers into service, often building their careers and attaining higher ranks, such as officers. With-in two generations many well-placed officers and the majority of the senior enlisted ranks of the Syrian Army were Nusayris. Being well placed in the Army served the Alawi well when the inevitable coups occurred as individuals jockeyed for power and attempted to consolidate their grip on the nation.

In the postcolonial period, a power vacuum occurred that the Army could not fill alone. The political situation also called for some type of political machine to aid in the consolidation of power. The machine that emerged was the Ba'ath party. The Syrians, "who formed the Ba'ath party, were committed to the unification of all Arabic-speaking peoples within a framework that would ensure individual freedom and build a socialist economy."[102] The initial goal of the Ba'ath party was to establish The United Arab Republic and, by popular vote, Syria and Egypt would have combined into a single nation. Saudi Arabia and Iraq were opposed to the idea and built a competing power block to stymie the plan. The idea of The United Arab Republic did not survive but the Ba'ath party remained and flourished in Syria and Iraq. In Syria, the Alawi began flocking to the Ba'ath party. "Nusayri officers began to claim that, more than any other officers, they were responsible for upholding the new government and that they were guardians of the

---

[101] Ibid., 293

[102] Arthur Goldschmidt Jr and Lawrence Davidson, *A Concise History of the Middle East*, 316.

Ba'ath party."[103] By taking over the Army and the major political party it was only a matter of time until the Alawi were able to assert their claim as leaders of the country.

The national take-over began slowly and then built momentum "The new Ba'ath Party, controlled by Nusayri strongmen, began systematically to purge and arrest Sunnite Muslims, Druzes, and Ismailis in the party and the Army."[104] Through the guise of the Ba'ath party and the military, the Alawi took control of the government in the shadows until 22 February 1971 when Hafiz al-Assad became the first Nusayri president of Syria.[105]

> The Nusayri community, which suffered discrimination, ridicule, rejection, and economic deprivation at the hands of the Sunnite Syrian majority, has evolved from a 'backward religious community to a nationally emancipated population group in a position of dominance.' Today, the Syrian government and army and indeed Syria's destiny, are in the hands of the Nusayri.[106]

This grassroots political insurgency of a repressed culture and religion has maintained power for 40 years now. This is an amazing feat considering the political volatility of the Middle East. Syria had previously experienced 15 coups and attempted coups from 1950 to 1970.[107]

The survival and the preeminence of the Ba'ath party in both Syria and Iraq put two men in power of their respective countries that were so similar that they hated each other - Hafiz al-Assad in Syria, and Saddam Hussein in Iraq. Their personal relationship forged, "one of the oldest and most bitter personal quarrels in the Middle East."[108] Each of these men came to power by overthrowing their respective governments, and maintained an iron grip on their societies through, violence, manipulation, and division. Both were Ba'ath party members, both vied for international leadership, and finally, both used family and clan ties to bolster their leadership

---

[103] Matti Moosa, *Extremist Shiites: The Ghulat Sects*, 299.

[104] Ibid., 305.

[105] Ibid., 309.

[106] Ibid, 310.

[107] Patrick Brogan, *World Conflicts: A Comprehensive Guide to World Strife Since 1945*, 366.

[108] Ibid., 371.

claims. [109] This personal hatred forged allies in the region that make diplomacy more difficult for western governments today.

Although Syria acted as an ally to the United States during Operation Desert Storm, the countries motives were not truly altruistic. Syria was more concerned with preventing Saddam Hussein from maintaining his claim on Kuwait, which would have directly challenged Syria's regional dominance. Moreover, in the Iran/Iraq war, Syria sided with Iran. Although both Iraq and Syria have Ba'athist roots, the relationship with Iraq faded and Syria's relationship with Iran strengthened.

The Syrian and Iranian alliance is unusual, but it has endured and strengthened over time. Several threads connect the two countries. On the political front, both countries are violently opposed to the United States and Israel. Economically Syria and Iran both experienced economic hardships in the guise of western sanctions. An article in The New York Times argued that "Syria was paralyzed by the Bush Administrations isolation policies, and had no other options than to turn to Iran; the Bush administration had unwittingly drawn the two "unnatural" allies closer together."[110] Moreover, the USSR was the provider for much of Syria's military material and training. After the collapse of the USSR in 1991, "Arms, subsidies and cheap oil were cut off all together."[111] This was a very challenging situation for Damascus and it forced the Alawi regime to find new benefactors to maintain its power. Iran stepped in to fill this void as well. However, it is not an easy alliance between Syria and Iran.

There are some significant differences between the two countries. Ideologically the two countries are not well matched and seem to be at odds. The contrasting ideologies are, "Syrian Pan-Arab nationalism/Ba'athism and Iranian Khomeini-style Islamic Revolution...the first is

---

[109] Ibid., 371.

[110] Tony Badran, inFocus Spring 2009 Volume III: Number 1, accessed March 16, 2010

[111] Patrick Brogan, *World Conflicts: A Comprehensive Guide to World Strife Since 1945*, 372.

seen as secular while the latter is theocratic."[112] Additionally, Iranians are Persian and predominantly Shia, while Syrians are Arab and predominantly Sunni. There is deep distrust between the Persians and Arabs and between Shia and Sunni. However, a minority Shia sect to which the Iranian Imams have provided legitimacy, governs Syria.

This overall sectarian split is an area that western militaries need to exploit. Strategically the United States is taking the first steps to facilitate an operational approach in Syria. President Barak Obama recently appointed Ambassador Robert S. Ford to the post in Damascus, and he has lifted travel restrictions with Syria. This opens the way for high-level talks to occur between the United States and Syria. Overall, the western isolationist approach toSyria has reduced the ability of the United States to leverage Syria and it has also forced a deepened connection with Iran. As a result of reopening of the American Embassy in Damascus, the military attaché will begin discourse with their Syrian counterparts. This discourse will facilitate operational opportunities. This is not a quick and easy path for western militaries to influence but at this point, there are no operational engagements occurring in Syria.

The goals of the operational approach in Syria are to aid in the peace process with Israel and degrade the growing regional power of Iran. Partnerships between western militaries and the Syrian military at the operational level will help foster these goals. Each year United States Army Central Command USARCENT hosts an event called the Land Forces Symposium. This is an opportunity for very senior military leaders from the Middle East, South and Central Asia to come together and generate substantial dialog about key issues, policy, military-to-military support, and build relationships. In 2010, the event was co-hosted by General George Casey, Chief of Staff of the United States Army, and Lieutenant General William Webster Commander Third United States Army and USARCENT. The inclusion of Syria in this event sets an

---

[112] Tony Badran, inFocus Spring 2009 Volume III: Number 1, accessed March 16, 2010

important precedence, as it offers opening broader military-to-military engagements and the dialog between the senior officers that allows for the determination of capabilities and priorities.

The importance of this interaction is that in the case of the Syrian senior military attendee, the officer will be a member of the minority Alawi sect of Shia. This minor fact would be missed by most Western militaries, however, it is certain that other Arab military leaders would recognize that this officer represents a religious minority with-in his society. The loss of the USSR as a benefactor of Syria and Iran's ability to step and become a new benefactor can be reversed through this military-to-military engagement. Western militaries can become benefactors to the Syrian military and work into a position to erode the support of Iran. Recognizing the minority rule, allowing the strengthening of that position by Alawi leaders, and trying to help Syria become more secular aids in our regional goals.

Conclusion

The history of the Middle East and splits in the Muslim religion offer levers to western militaries to exploit operational and strategic opportunities. Often these opportunities go unrealized because our militaries are unfamiliar with the history that formed sectarian splits in the Muslim religion. By tracing the steps of these conflicts can we determine cause and affect relationships and see a complex system how it exists. The split between the Sunni and Shia is one of the greatest rifts in our modern society and it is playing an increasingly larger role on the world stage. Western militaries operating in the Middle East today make frequent missteps as a result of the lack of fundamental knowledge about the societies in which they interact.

In Yemen, the Shia Imamates lost power decades ago, yet an underlying tension still exists that causes a minor insurgency in the northern areas of the country. Western Armies have military advisors embedded in the Yemeni Special Forces, and one of the lines of effort these forces should exploit is the sectarian line of effort. Reconciling the al-Houthi in the north with the Government of Yemen would help to stabilize the Government and allow a more detailed engagement of the GoY Forces against al-Queda Arabian Peninsula (AQAP). Moreover, the Shia al-Houthi can leverage additional intelligence gathering against AQAP in an effort of self-protection. The goals of western militaries in Yemen coincide with the goals of both the al-Houthi Tribe and the Government of Yemen. It is imperative operationally that western militaries begin to exploit this sectarian rift and aid in the repair of the nation to the best interests of all parties. However, the operational approach used in one country or region cannot be universally applied and each instance requires individual study to determine appropriate courses of action.

Syria poses a much different problem for western militaries, as a minority-led government that claims it is secular. However, history clearly demonstrates that sectarian issues motivated the Alawi grab for power. Western militaries, and more specifically, the United States, find themselves on the outside through a policy of isolation. Ironically, isolation created the exact issues that the United States hoped to avoid.

The question posed is how to use sectarian levers to reverse the trend of the growing Shia influence in the Iran/Iraq/Syria crescent and encourage Syria re-engagement into the Middle East Peace Process. At the strategic level, the re-establishment of the United States Embassy in Damascus is a huge step. Operationally, we should begin with a military-to-military engagement. This could occur at a minor level by inviting the Syrian Army Chief of Staff to the United States Army Central Command Land Forces Symposium. This small effort could open opportunities to begin operational interaction with Syrian Military forces. Key to this is understanding that the head of the Syrian Military will not be a Sunni Officer, as would be the case in most every other Arab-led military force. Instead, the head of the Syrian Army will be an Alawi Shia. This nuance would not be recognized by most western personnel, the other Muslim attendees of the Symposium would be keenly aware of it. Although regime change may not be what we desire in Syria, there is a clear need for support and subsidies, and Syria has demonstrated that it will provide some loyalty to its benefactors.

BIBLIOGRAPHY

Allawi, Dr. Ali A. *The Crisis of Islamic Civilization*. New York, NY.: Yale University Press, 2009.

Amos, Deborah. *Eclipse of the Sunnis: Power, Exile, and Upheaval in the Middle East*. New York: PublicAffairs, 2010.

Barber, Benjamin. *Jihad vs. McWorld: Terrorism's Challenge to Democracy*. Edition Unstated ed. New York: Ballantine Books, 1996.

Benjamin, Daniel, and Steven Simon. *The Age of Sacred Terror*. New York: Random House, 2002.

Bonney, Richard. *False Prophets (The Past in the Present)*. Hong Kong: Peter Lang, 2008.

Brogan, Patrick. *World Conflicts: A Comprehensive Guide to World Strife Since 1945*. 3 Sub ed. Lanham, Md.: The Scarecrow Press, Inc., 1999.

Bush, George W. "The War and Caring from American Soldiers: Remarks at the American Legion 47th National Conference", Presidential Rheroric.com, http://www.presidentialrhetoric.com/speeches/03.06.07.html (accessed November 18, 2010)

Burns, John F., "Efforts to Avert Sectarian Reprisals After Shrine Attack" New York Times, http://www.nytimes.com/2007/06/14/world/middleeast/14iraq.html (accessed November 14, 2010)

Cole, Juan. *Sacred Space And Holy War: The Politics, Culture and History of Shi'ite Islam*. London: I. B. Tauris, 2002.

Collins English Dictionary – Complete & Unabridged 10th Edition, "Sectarianism", Dictionary.Com, http://dictionary.reference.com/browse/Sectarianism (accessed November 18, 2010)

Donner, Fred M. *Muhammad and the Believers: At the Origins of Islam*. New York: Belknap Press of Harvard University Press, 2010.

Early Bird, http://ebird.osd.mil/ebfiles/e20110117800462.html, 60 Minutes transcript Aired January 16, 2011, accessed January 18,, 2011

Fakhry, Majid. *Islamic Philosophy: A Beginner's Guide (Beginners Guide (Oneworld))*. Reprint ed. Oxford: Oneworld, 2009.

Fox, Jonathan. *Religion, Civilization, and Civil War: 1945 through the New Millennium*. Cambridge: Lexington Books, 2004.

Fox, Jonathan, and Shmuel Sandler. *Bringing Religion into International Relations (Culture and Religion in International Relations)*. New York: Palgrave Macmillan, 2004.

Fuller, Graham E., and Rend Rahim Francke. *The Arab Shi'a: The Forgotten Muslims*. New York: Palgrave Macmillan, 2001.

Gerner, Deborah J. *One Land, Two Peoples: The Conflict Over Palestine (Dilemmas in World Politics)*. Boulder: Westview Press, 1990.

Global Security.org. "Samarra", John Pike, http://www.globalsecurity.org/military/world/iraq/samarra-mosque.htm (accessed November 18, 2010)

Halm, Heinz, and Allison Brown. *Shi'a Islam: From Religion to Revolution (Princeton Series on the Middle East)*. Princeton, NJ.: Markus Wiener Publishers, 1996.

Hazleton, Lesley. *After the Prophet: The Epic Story of the Shia-Sunni Split in Islam*. New York: Anchor, 2010

Hunter, Shireen T. *The Future of Islam and the West: Clash of Civilizations or Peaceful Coexistence?* Westport, Conn.: Praeger Publishers, 1998.

Huntington, Samuel P. *The Clash of Civilizations and the Remaking of World Order*. New York: Simon & Schuster, 1998.

Islamic Occasions, "Second Infallible Ali (AS) the First Imam", Islamic Occasions: Truth Wisdom and Justice. http://www.ezsoftech.com/islamic/infallible2a.asp, (accessed December 21, 2101)

Jafri, S. Husain M. *Origins and Early Development in Shi'a Islam (Arab Background Series)*. London: Longman Group United Kingdom, 2000.

Jr, Arthur Goldschmidt, and Lawrence Davidson. *A Concise History of the Middle East*. Eighth Edition, Eighth Edition ed. Boulder, CO.: Westview Press, 2005.

Katzenstein, Peter J., ed. *The Culture of National Security: Norms and Identity in World Politics (New Directions in World Politics)*. Chichester: Columbia University Press, 1996.

Landler, Mark and Cooper, Helene, "Obama Speech Signals a U.S. Shift on the Middle East", NY Times, 14 April 2010

Lapidus, Ira M. *Contemporary Islamic Movements in Historical Perspective (Policy Papers in International Affairs)*. New York: Univ of California Inst of, 1983.

Lee, Robert D. *Overcoming Tradition And Modernity: The Search For Islamic Authenticity*. Chichester: Westview Press, 1997.

Lewis, Bernard. *From Babel to Dragomans: Interpreting the Middle East*. 1ST ed. Chichester: Oxford University Press, USA, 2004.

Lewis, Bernard. *What Went Wrong?: The Clash Between Islam and Modernity in the Middle East*. Hong Kong: Harper Perennial, 2003.

Lincoln, Bruce, ed. *Religion, Rebellion, Revolution: An Inter-Disciplinary and Cross-Cultural Collection of Essays*. Hong Kong: Palgrave Macmillan, 1985.

Little, David, and Donald K. Swearer, eds. *Religion and Nationalism in Iraq: A Comparative Perspective (Studies in World Religions)*. Chichester: Center for the Study of World Religions, 2007.

McFate, Montgomery, "*The Military Utility of Understanding Adversary Culture*", Joint Forces Quarterly, 38, (2005): 44

Mill, John Stuart, *A System of Logic: Ratiocinative and Inductive*, 8th ed. (New York: Harper & Brothers Publishing, 1904), 280

Moosa, Matti. *Extremist Shiites: The Ghulat Sects (Contemporary Issues in the Middle East)*. Syracuse: Syracuse University Press, 1988.

Nasr, Vali. *The Shia Revival: How Conflicts within Islam Will Shape the Future*. New York: W. W. Norton, 2006.

Nydell, Margaret K. *Understanding Arabs: A Guide for Modern Times*. 4th Edition ed. New York: Nicholas Brealey Boston, 2005.

Mackey, Sandra, and Scott Harrop. *The Iranians: Persia, Islam and the Soul of a Nation*. New York: Plume, 1998.

Reuda, David, "How to Compare Countries Lecture 2", Oxford University, http://webcache.googleusercontent.com/search?q=cache:xO1S8Yt86k4J:users.ox.ac.uk/~polf0050/Rueda%2520How%2520to%2520Compare%2520Countries%2520Lecture%25202.ppt+przeworski+most+different+systems&cd=2&hl=en&ct=clnk&gl=us , (Accessed November 21, 2010)

Rustow, Dankwart A., and Kenneth P. Erickson. *Comparative Political Dynamics: Global Research Perspectives*. Chichester: Harpercollins College Div, 1990.

Salmoni, Barak A., Bryce Loidolt, and Madeleine Wells. *Regime and Periphery in Northern Yemen: The Huthi Phenomenon*. Santa Monica, CA.: Rand Publishing, 2010.

Smith, Lee. *The Strong Horse: Power, Politics, and the Clash of Arab Civilizations*. New York: Doubleday, 2010.

Sunna.org, "http://www.sunnah.org/articles/Wahhabiarticleedit.htm", by Zubair Qamar, accessed on 07 Feb 2011.

Takim, Liyakat. *Shi'ism in America*. New York: NYU Press, 2009.

Tamimi, Azzam. *Hamas: A History from Within*. Northampton, Mass.: Olive Branch Press, 2007.

Tucker, William F. *Mahdis and Millenarians: Shiite Extremists in Early Muslim Iraq*. New York: Cambridge University Press, 2008.

Turabian, Kate L. *A Manual for Writers of Research Papers, Theses, and Dissertations*. 7th ed. Chicago: University of Chicago Press, 2007.

Youngblood-Coleman, Denise, editor. *Country Review: Syria. 2010*. Houston, Texas: CountryWatch Publications, 2010. Country Review:Syria. Online. Available URL: http://www.countrywatch.com/cw_country.aspx?vcountry=167, accessed October, 12, 2010.

Youngblood-Coleman, Denise, editor. *Country Review: Yemen. 2010*. Houston, Texas: CountryWatch Publications, 2010. Country Review: Yemen. Online. Available URL: http://www.countrywatch.com/cw_country.aspx?vcountry=188, accessed October, 12, 2010.